AF576963

Rabbit of the Nether World

Reiko Koyanagi

Illustrated by Monica Tamano

Translated by Hiroaki Sato

Rabbit of the Nether World

ISBN 1-893959-01-5

Red Moon Press
P.O. Box 2461
Winchester VA
22604-1661 USA

Originally appeared as *Yomi no Usagi*
published by Kashinsha, in 1989.

Table of Contents

Preface

Reiko Koyanagi's book *Yomi no Usagi*, here translated as *Rabbit of the Nether World*, describes the author's experience of the Second World War through a collage of poems and prose.

Koyanagi, who was born in 1935, contracted a severe case of tuberculosis toward the end of the war and, in the worsening food shortages and 'frying pan' bombings that afflicted Japan, had to struggle through a twilight zone. At one time she looked so hopelessly wasted that her father made her a coffin out of an orange crate. Death was ever present. Throughout this small memoir a rabbit reminiscent of the one in *Alice's Adventures in Wonderland* shows up as the beckoner to the nether world.

Yet *Rabbit of the Nether World* is not so much about the allure of death remembered from a ravaged childhood as about the first awareness of love experienced and the discovery later of its emptiness.

Love first occurs for the poet's father. He was a mathematician, 'original' enough to be asked by the Imperial Navy to work out "differential equations for ballistic calculations for rockets" and to be included after the war in an *Encyclopedia of Mathematics*. Living nonetheless in dire poverty during this period, he—a man whose wife had walked out on him for her lover—delighted in teaching mathematics to his daughter while taking care of her. Still, after the war, when he, by then a prominent corporate executive, was asked to serialize an autobiographical account for a leading economic daily, he recollected things like the final futility of his ballistic computations (by the time he completed them, the Empire of Japan had no more rockets), but said not a word about his days with his daughter. This hurt.

The other disillusionment is of a different kind. With the war over, the father leaves the village where he has taken refuge. Pulling a cart carrying his emaciated daughter, he passes by a farmhouse and is given a sizable amount of rice by the mistress of the house, who profoundly sympathizes with the girl. And the girl, though in feverish delirium, remembers the name of the kind farmer and the crepe myrtle growing in the garden. Years later, she visits the village to express her gratitude and, perhaps, convey her love to the kindly woman. But she finds out that practically every family in the area has the same surname and a crepe myrtle planted in their garden.

Before *Rabbit of the Nether World*, Koyanagi published five books of poems, beginning with *Mieteiru Mono (What Remains Visible)*, in 1966. Reading them, one observes certain things: Koyanagi is haunted by an odd group of ghost-like uncles and aunts; some of her books repeat pieces from earlier ones; and she apparently wrote each of her books to rid herself of some demon. In *Rabbit of the Nether World*, these traits converge: the supporting characters are the poet's aunts and uncles; several poems are carried over from the book that precedes it, *Tsukiyo no Shigoto (Work on a Moonlit Night)*, of 1983; and the demon to be rid of is the lack or aimlessness of love.

Rabbit of the Nether World is also the best of Koyanagi's books up to that time. It tells the story of exorcising a demon most coherently, and it has some amusing descriptions. For example, toward the end of the narrative, the rabbit observes: "It was long ago, there was a war. This town also had an air raid and was surrounded by fires. I tell you, it was terrible. Burning a small rural town like this, well, I bet the other side had an awful lot of excess bombs." Perhaps this ability to be amused at one's situation is a sign of liberation.

Yomi no Usagi was published by Kashinsha, in 1989, and awarded the Poets' Club prize in 1990. Koyanagi's other books are: *Takan na Chijō (Sensitive Ground)*, by Gendaishi Kōbō, in 1971; *Ashi no Sato kara (From a Reed Village)*, by Kashinsha, in 1976; *Oba-san no Ie (Aunt's House)*, by Komagome Shobō, in 1980; *Kumogaoka Densetsu (Clouds Hill Legend)*, by Shichōsha, in 1993; and *Kodomo no Ryōbun (A Child's Realm)*, by Kashinsha, in 1997.

I am grateful to Nancy Rossiter and Robert Fagan for helping me edit this translation.

Hiroaki Sato
New York City

Rabbit of the Nether World

—Summer 1989

While in town I suddenly found that entrance to the subway. It is really rare to see its dim stairway. Long ago, I once saw it below my apartment on a hill, but by the time I put on my sandals and went down, it was gone. No, a friend had spoken to me, and I was saying things like, "Hi, how are you?" After that I moved countless times, and I had forgotten about it.

I purchased a ticket to Village in a hurry. It's one of my pleasures, remarkably enough, to get on a train to go nowhere, aimlessly. I found out that the subway went down to a place rather deep. See, floating up there was that dirty moon that comes out underground.

All the passengers were tinted like smoke, and the moment you thought they were ballooning, they visibly shrank, sometimes singing, "Twilight Cat, Good Evening." Past Forest and Broom stations, I slept a little. I got off at Village. The terminal. As in the past, that skinny rabbit was taking the tickets. "How did you manage to come?" He was staring at me as if surprised.

"Oh, it was nothing"—I said, embarrassed—I just got on the train that happened to come by.

"But there isn't even one train a year bound for this place, no?" He was staring at me with that mysterious, gentle face as if he were sorry that I had wasted my time. Then he said something like what follows, though I'm afraid there may be some points that I misunderstood.

If you don't have somebody you want to see, it's useless to come to visit here. Besides, you must desperately love that somebody.

(Can you desperately love somebody, a human being . . .?)

"Otherwise, this is just the underground. Look at the houses. The doors and windows are shut. Look at the nameplates, too. You can't read any of the names.

Of course, sometimes there are names you feel you may have glimpsed. But you can't remember. Everybody's asleep. You make their sleep deeper. You know, someone who has never loved with all her heart can't find that subway in the first place. You are a strange person, aren't you?

(Yes, no matter where I go, people tell me I'm a strange person.)

Can it be that you are looking for the memory that you once did love, I wonder? If that isn't the case, you are trying to do something all over again, aren't you?

A small, feeble moon was walking in the sky. A very aged moon. Its thin light was crying *yoyoyoyo yoyoyoyo* as it fell into a ditch. I recognized the house by the ditch. The name on its nameplate resembled the one that I had once loved in my own way. But as I brought my face close to it, it resembled the name of the one I had fiercely loathed one year. Blinking my eyes, I was getting closer to the house or going away from it. In the old amusement park the Ferris wheel that had stopped long ago was looking down toward me. Mickey Mouse, Snow White, and others were laughing, hands thrown up, mouths wide open.

I got on the last train. The loudspeaker of the station was persistently shouting, "All passengers, please do not turn back to look.

"No matter who calls to you, please don't turn back to look. If you do turn back, you won't be able to come back. Do be careful."

But no one called to me.

Only the enfeebled moon followed me to Broom station. The moon had grown so weak it collapsed in the sky like a piece of rag. Then Forest.

Still, no one ever called to me.

At the place where I got off the train, I purchased cigarettes. When I was lighting one, I met a friend of mine.

"Hi," he said.

"Hi, I haven't seen you for a long time." I had been on the verge of remembering something, but it was too much trouble. It seems I had decided to forget about it.

"How've you been doing? Since that time?" I said something like this.

—Once Upon a Time

I'd like to begin with the story of flowing-water calculations. It was near the end of summer. A strong westerly sun was flooding into the room. The tiny room felt as if it were immersed in the westerly sun.

I was a second grader at national school.† I was solving 'flow-water' calculus. Somehow I had a degree of talent in mathematics. I wrote diagrams and childish equations everywhere, on the walls that were stained all over and on the orange crate that I used as my desk.

Roasted by the westerly sun, these had become distinct, looking as if they were about to wriggle out and march toward me like deformed dwarfs.

Mathematics was to be a useless talent for me all my life. Yet it was a talent that would hurt me with almost palpable pain.

I was solving flowing-water calculations. Late summer. Father, who was a destitute mathematician, was, on any day and intently, trying to put statistical tables in order. In those days I was convinced that "Father," in any house, was solving mathematical formulas. Father, who seldom indulged in dreams, had nonetheless the faint dream of making a mathematician out of me, but that dream was always blocked by thorns and bitter pills. Early dead zelkova leaves, mingling with the westerly sun, were blown one after another onto the figures that Father and I wrote.

† In 1941 all the *shōgakkō* (lit., "small schools," *i.e.*, elementary or primary schools) were renamed *kokumin gakkō* (lit., "national schools")—evidently in an attempt to reproduce German *Volksschule.* The name reverted to the original one in 1947.

—Father, is there a numeral that doesn't exist anywhere in the world? I asked.

—I don't mean something that is very bulky or very small, but a numeral that can't *be*, that's what I mean.

How did Father reply? I have no memory. Except until very late that night Father kept laughing to himself. That day ended like that.

—Tablecloth

I should also talk about Rabbit early on. Though it's an odd rabbit that I became friendly with when I was five or six years old. He was white—though, well, rabbits are mostly white—and was perched at the left edge of the tablecloth. The cloth was light green, probably representing a grassfield. The flowers, which were red and blue, were terribly simple. At the center of the cloth was a plain two-storied house. The first floor had a kitchen and a dining room. The second floor was a tiny room for a girl. Somehow I knew that was the way it was.

The appearances of both flowers and clouds there were pleasant. The air was clean and dry. Above all, things that are incredible now, such as love, filled the windows and oven as if they were real.

In this design only red-eyed Rabbit looking sideways was inauspicious.

"—Well, all I do is eat chickweed, you know.—" He often said that, but that was hardly enough of an excuse. First, he had a distinct shadow. When none of the things there, even the house or the trees, cast a shadow. His shadow at times looked like a deep hole. Or, in the poor light at night, it looked like the large face of a man. Father was laughing. The saurel broiled with salt had turned into a head and bones. The night meal was finished. A great many night meals were finished like that. The cloth grew dirty, and I don't remember when, but it was cut into small squares. It turned into rags for wiping shoes. Under where the cloth used to be, there were three orange crates lined up side by side—a distant memory. Because they formed the dining table of my house. Anyway, as a result, Rabbit ceased to be. From then on he would only occasionally show up in this world, looking sideways. I had decided to say my own good night to him only when I heard someone laughing in some distant corner.

—*Autumn*

In a corner of my dream there often were Rabbit's ears. He was also in the mirror at daybreak. In the slender looking-glass hung in the triangular room on the second floor—perhaps because of the space allocation, that room formed an odd triangle—Rabbit was walking slowly or, sometimes, restively, like a shadow. In the living room below, Mother was chattering in her high-pitched voice. Autumn was noisily falling on the roof of that poor house, on its rain-doors. Mother chatted about my looks and my talent, and Father tended to remain silent. Rabbit, somewhere deep in the wall, was pricking up his ears. I knew he was.

Mathematics was making me more and more unhappy, Mother seemed to believe. In the thick autumn that was noisily piling up, I remained standing.

—If a *pumpkin*-like girl like that became a *mathematician*, who would take her as a bride?

Pumpkin! Pumpkin! Mother cried several times, angrily.

I learned for the first time that a pumpkin was something resembling me.

Autumn was falling with thuds. Because of those crude sounds, things were disturbed in my dreams.

—Rabbit. I called. He wasn't there. Only the black hole through which he'd left was visible. I'll go down there someday. I'd like to tell you about it. About a small straw-sandal I picked up there, and about that white coffin that transfigures itself night by night. Someday.

—*Living*

By the time the Second World War began to list and sink in Japan's defeat, Father no longer had any means of income left. I can't accurately talk about the degree of his talent as a mathematician, but several years ago Iwanami Shoten got in touch with me about him. Judging from the fact that the prestigious publisher planned to include his name and an entry on his achievements in its *Encyclopedia of Mathematics*, we might say that his talent had some originality.

But regardless of his talent, poverty was invading our house like water. Ours could no longer be called a living.

Green vines, butterflies, infected leaves, winged insects, endlessly entered the house from the verandah. In the earth floor of the entrance frogs and slugs had begun to live, with no intention of leaving.

Rabbit, who was invisible to Father, also came to visit from a hole in the wall or from the case for the slide rule. He was as small as a snail, you thought, but another day he was a flat, gigantic shadow that covered the whole ceiling.

The night meal was mostly a light soup with grass leaves cooked in it. With one excuse or another I would bring home, for Father, the tough, tasteless loaf of bread given as school lunch at elementary school. The two of us, Father and I, would bloat it in the soup and finish our meal.

On such nights, Rabbit would be found in the kitchen. He was drifting through the night like smoke. Or was washing invisible rice, plenty of it. As his hands moved in the air, the whole darkness that packed the kitchen felt like an unimaginably large pot.

—*Mathematical Expressions*

After that, ferocious days of air raids began. Because father and daughter had no place to escape to, they continued to live outside Tokyo, not knowing what else to do.

Because of the blackout and poverty we rarely used electricity. In the evening light Father taught me mathematical expressions. I was in third grade. Father explained square roots and imaginary numbers as he wrote their symbols on a sheet of straw paper. I continued to solve those given me.

—This is the number you've been looking for. Father said.

—The number that can't exist anywhere.

I probably kept silent.

But, Father, isn't there any equation that represents this hunger and these endless war-fires? Can't you factorize them? Father continued to feverishly talk about geniuses in the mathematical world, such as Galois, Weierstrass, and Abel.

—Father, wasn't there a mathematical expression that would keep Mother's heart moored to yours? Last night Mother was sewing a new pair of women's trousers throughout the night. She must have been making them out of a party dress she had as a young woman. Today she put them on and went out. You know where she went, don't you, Father?

In exchange for my pumpkin-like looks, my parents gave me a brain that probably resembled my father's. With uncanny speed I went on understanding the algebra and geometry that in his excitement he taught me.

Father's dream expanded to such an extent that he mistook my cold eyes for sharpness.

—Father, can you express your unhappiness through a mathematical formula? Father, your notebook doesn't have any diagram that proves that rabbit, does it? Your formulas can't express any dimension that Rabbit and I can get in. No matter how loud we scream, you can't hear the language of the country of Rabbit and me.

During a rainy season I developed a high fever and took to bed. It was malnutrition. Every night I would wander into an indeterminate land. I'd like to tell you about it. If possible, about a tiny old woman, about the coffin on a moonlit night, about the staircase that leads to the nether world.

—*Illnesses*

About the months and days when poverty surrounded my house and flourished like vines, I told you yesterday. The people called "illnesses" constantly came to my body and lodged in it for several days at a time. There were about six of them, and they were shaped like extremely small human beings. It was thought they lived deep in the wall on the north side. In the rainy season—as you also know, during this season walls turn into transparent gray liquid and waver—they sat in the wall, in a circle. You could see their white, skinny teeth as they chewed on bones.

"Brothers," some days I would hear one of the older ones call to his friends.

"Pour me some black milk."

He was in an excellent mood and was raising his voice further— "The damned blood is still left, plenty of it. Even in a shadowy child, too."

—*Father*

In 1944, Father's job was to make calculations commissioned by the Ministry of the Navy. For him that was the only job that led to any income.

One day the room was filled with the noise of an electric calculator. This old-fashioned, oil-smelling, coal-black machine is making rickety-rackety sounds even now, in my dream, if I go into a room like, say, a basement. Father's job was to compute the angle and speed for a dropped bomb to hit an enemy battleship. Dizzy, endless numbers spewed out of the machine and piled up on the floor.

A light darkness began to fall on the numbers, a darker ceiling on the darkness, and on top of the ceiling the deep face of the rainy season. The small room of Father and me drifted through the rain, destination unknowable.

On nights when my fever was high, I would go through a long corridor as I fell into Rabbit Country. That giant man in the constellation Cowherd† glowed orange as he slowly sank toward the western edge.

—Spring 1945

The air raids were growing fierce. My house in a suburb of Tokyo was no longer safe. Every night, because of the blackout, we put a black wrapping cloth around the electric bulb, and in that semi-darkness we spent our time listening to the radio.

An uncle, a total stranger to me, suddenly materialized, looking like a skinny European dog in that meager light.

"Hi."

As he took his seat near the wall where Rabbit crouched, he cast a quick glance at me.

"She has a high fever. She asks for cider, but I can't get any." Rabbit was listening to Father explaining diffidently. He was looking up at Uncle with an air of distrust, but of course, both to Uncle and Father he, a gray shadow, was invisible.

Knowing well that the relationship between Father and Mother had turned sour and that Mother no longer was in this house, Mother's younger brother had come to visit, now in a feminine voice pleading with Father to share a certain drug with him.

"If I had some of it," said Uncle—I could get hold of rice and sugar, I could bring a mountainous amount of rice."

The drug that Uncle wanted to get from Father's close friend, a doctor, was, come to think of it now, penicillin. At the time it didn't have that name yet, and must have been in an experimental stage.

My mother, who couldn't boast anything about her husband, must have boasted about his friend who was on the verge of developing a drug that could cure septicemia. Trusting that story, Uncle had come with the intention of making a small fortune.

† Aquila, though "Cowherd" (*Ushikai-za* or *Kengyū-za*) often refers to the brightest star in the constellation, Altair.

What looked like sad resignation spread over Father's face, and disappeared at once. He must have written a letter of introduction to his friend. Uncle must have left to get penicillin, of which there must have been only several vials' worth at the time.

As he stepped down the staircase, Uncle shouted, "Yes, rice, mountains of it!"

"Cider for Reiko, too . . . you know!"

For a while Father watched Uncle from the window on the second floor. An air raid siren had begun to sound. Uncle's skinny back must have turned the corner at the store of western suits. It must have disappeared, before you had time to bat an eye, behind the shrine, further into the sparse wood behind it.

Besides, Uncle had left his running shoes, wearing Father's leather shoes instead as he left. Neither the shoes nor Uncle returned to the house, not once.

Rabbit, looking sad, kept his face leaning on my chest for a long time. That's why I knew that cider would never reach me. Only Father waited for it forever. Each time he heard the sound of glass bottles, he would hurry to the door and stand there, his face exposed to the moonlight, blank.

—The Small Room

On nights when my fever was particularly high, I would follow the skinny rabbit and walk through the narrow corridor. The corridor gradually tapered and collapsed deep into the night. Each time we turned a corner, we would run into a small shrine. A fox appeared to be enshrined. Then that small room would inevitably emerge. In order to get in the room the size of a knapsack, I would melt like wax.

A small chair, a small table, also a small plate with a spoon.

In the darkness of the room was a teeny, tiny old woman cooking cabbage.

"Welcome, you," she would say in a reedy voice.

"Eat the soup, eat plenty of it."

The soup was poured endlessly into the darkness at my feet and would never fill the plate. She gradually grew large, ballooning to fill the room; in the darkness cabbage was being cooked.

Don't worry, eat your soup.

You're wondering who I am, aren't you? I'm always with you. I've been with you since long before you were born. Eat the soup. Now, and way into the future as well.

In the evening, sparrows and frogs are looking intently at you.

Somehow you feel very gentle.

At such a time, I am near you.

You want to call to someone, or you want to write a letter,
but you don't remember to whom, you stay still holding a pencil;
at such a time, I am by you.

Somewhere in the night a flag flaps, you stop to listen,
I've arrived.

Outside the town, the lamp at the gate of a house turns on, and as if a signal the lamp at every gate is lit; there's a gate without a nameplate, and for a while you're looking at the second floor of that house, and something is about to be remembered;
at such a time I'm with you, I tell you.

When you are putting tin plates on the table, your hand suddenly slips, I am by you.

When you sleep, when you wake up at midnight briefly,
when you laugh in your dreams, I've arrived where you are.

Eat your soup.
She said in a reedy, distant voice.

I crossed a soup-like river.
Somewhere the 7 o'clock news had begun.

> —Bulletin from the Middle Military District HQ: *285 enemy U.S. B-29's invaded Japan in three groups beginning at 2100 hours on the 5th.*

We crossed a swamp.
Nuphars were abloom all over the swamp like lights.
Where am I going I asked.
"Far, far away," someone said.

> *—Some of the bombers dropped mines in parts of the Japan Sea and the Inland Sea, while the third group of 130 bombers dropped incendiary bombs in the Nishinomiya City area and in some parts dropped a mixture of incendiaries and bombs.*

While passing by the cedar wood, I came across Rabbit.
"Farther away," he said.
I climbed a mist-like ladder.
Somewhere in the night a flag was flapping.
I couldn't remember something.

> *—The fires in the Nishinomiya City area were put out as a result of the heroic efforts of both the military and non-military people before daybreak on the 6th. While investigations of our damages are still under way—*

Rabbit had turned into a round tin plate
and was hanging in the western sky.
The flag was flapping, and I couldn't remember.
The 7 o'clock news was about to end.

—the damages we inflicted that were ascertained by ten o'clock on the 6th include eight bombers shot down.
We will follow this with Mozart's wind and string composition, "A Little Night Music," performed by the Tokyo Symphony Orchestra.

—Constellation Cowherd

Father and I loved a somewhat amorphous constellation called the Cowherd. During the rainy season, on rare occasions when the rains let up, we sometimes saw the stars in the evening sky. The Cowherd, an enormous man with a dog, would slowly descend toward the west, side by side with the constellation Hair. Father was constantly mumbling figure-like things, like thirty, forty. They may have been fragments of the mathematical formulas he'd been thinking about for over a year. Almost all the time his head was occupied by formulas related to ellipses.

I was always with Rabbit. For I tended to be ill and didn't have any friend. He would call to me from behind in a clear voice, at times in a voice that couldn't be called a voice. We, along with Father, would look up at the star and the sky from the laundry-drying deck. In our air-raid hoods, in the lightless night.

Both the legs and the chest of the Cowherd had sunk beyond the forest. With only his face afloat above night's forest, he would remain looking intently, as if with some regrets, at our small house.

—Sound

The job from the Ministry of the Navy didn't seem to be making progress. It wasn't that Father wasn't eager about the work. For he loved his country. Probably he never once thought it would be better for us to lose the war. It's just that he was more deeply involved in his own mathematics than in the Navy Ministry job. Ignoring all such phenomena, though, heavy dark time was avalanching toward us to reach our house, which was unworthy of the name of house. To me, the one wasted to skin and bones, what sounded like quiet steps, as time piled up, were suffocating.

—I

In the moist darkness I asked.

"Father. What are the mathematical formulas you're thinking of meant to express?"

—I can't explain them to a grade-school child, Father replied.

"But you can say they express, for example, something pointless or express something that's important to you but not so important to Mother, or a different degree of importance to each. Or that the same rabbit has been turned into a silver plate in the country beyond. Express such things with equations, see."

Father seemed startled, speechless. But at once he regained his usual calm voice.

—They're totally different things, he replied.

"You are trembling like this in the air raid shelter, but can still be thinking of something other than death, can't you?" I probably asked something like that. Maybe in very different words.

—Whether you think about it or not, death comes to you as it pleases, Father said. My formulas will remain forever in the dark unless I think about them. That's all, you see. Except you can't say all of them are good once you drag them out of the dark, the way this world is. There are those beautifully asleep in the dark.

"Aren't you afraid of dying?"

—I am. I am terribly afraid. But I am even more afraid of your dying. When I'm *in* mathematics, I can sometimes forget—that I must keep you alive. I can even say now forgetting that may be the happiest thing for me.

—The Air Raid

That night, flare bombs were dropped in our town. The small town became brighter than the day. The dark air raid shelter also became full of mysterious brightness.

"Come here."

Someone said abruptly. A delicate cold hand pressed my wrist. On the earth wall deep on the further side of the moat that wasn't visible until moments ago was a faint suggestion of Rabbit.

"Don't go out," he said. Father couldn't hear Rabbit, but soon he was unable to go out either. Terrorized by all that brightness, he was about to go out, despite himself, when I fell down unconscious. Because of a sudden high fever I was violently shaking. "Don't go out," he said. The oval curves had faded into the distance, in the sky, like a bridge. At the very end of it, the Cowherd was laughing dryly, joyfully.—Don't go out.

That's how Father and I saved our lives. That night, in our small town, bombs and incendiaries were dropped in a manner that can only be called wild, and the whole town turned into a burnt-out field except for a section surrounding a marsh. Our room, left unburnt, was full of the smell of burst bombs for days on end.

—Bread

The morning after an air raid was over, Father went to a neighboring town. He returned with a lump of the steamed bread distributed to air-raid victims.

Sitting near my pillow he divided the still hot bread into two. He gave me the larger half, and ate the other half himself. He gobbled up the whole thing in about three bites.

Because of the fever and chill I was unable to eat.

"Let's keep yours until your fever goes away," Father said.

But he was unable to do that. Mumbling hardly audible words of apology, he put half of my bread into his mouth. Then he puffed up his cheeks with the remainder. It didn't take a minute. For his stomach that had received only radish leaves and a single slice of dried fish for the last two, three days, the steamed bread was too little. When the last piece of bread went down his throat, he wept incomparably sadly.

Let's go to Valley of Winds, Father said. It was his home town that he was supposed never to step in again.

—*The Night Train*

At Ueno Station barely left standing in the midst of a vast stretch of land where everything had been reduced to ashes, we waited for a train probably for nearly two days. Throngs of victims, by the hundreds, lingered on the ground like thrown-out rags, waiting for their trains.

The sun set, the sun rose, again the air raid siren sent out a warning. But we no longer had the will or energy to run about to save our lives, as we looked up at the sky, aimlessly waiting. Near noon, a woman who was squatting next to us gave me a handful of roasted soybeans. I divided them in half with Father and ate them.

In the evening we got on the train. The space we found must have been the connecting platform between cars. The rubberized protector was torn, and between the ribs you could see the track and crossties. We had to wait for several more hours before the train finally started. Below us the rails flowed back, continuously, like a white, sharp river.

Summer was near, but the night was cold.

From time to time I fell into a brief sleep.

In a corner of the sleep was Rabbit. He looked far more like a rabbit than usual and was lovely. He was silent. Even so, I was encouraged and happy beyond words.

No matter when I woke up, the train seemed to be running through the same darkness. Crouched next to me, Father was writing nonstop mathematical formulas with his finger on his palm.

—$\varnothing_x$

—$\varnothing'_x$

Father kept on mumbling.

I put in my mouth the remainder of the roasted soybeans that I'd been holding tightly in my hand. They were bitter and hard. The summer that was about to come would prove even more bitter and unbearably hard.

—Summer

How we reached Valley of Winds after that, my memory isn't certain. Somewhere at a station I was given a rice-ball the size of a child's head. Somehow only the memories of food are vivid.

Be that as it may, in an old house in a valley where the sounds of wind never ceased, our entire clan was to spend the summer. Uncles and an aunt died during the summer, one after another. About to be counted among the dead, I simply went on sleeping, Rabbit and I holding each other. The high fever, suppuration, and malnutrition bored a swamp-like hole in my body, and the hole kept expanding.

That old summer, though, already held in its deep chest many a new summer that was soon to come around. It had a faint, blue smell. And the many new summers would always hold this old summer in their chests as they came around to me feverishly, passionately.

—Valley of Winds

Father and I ran away to a village called Valley of Winds. Hounded by the war-fires and hunger, Father, with me in his custody, a child with tuberculosis, had no choice but to take refuge in his home town, a place that he loathed more fiercely than anything else. Mother had left him for her lover and hadn't come back. The only fortunate thing was that at the time family members living separately did not arouse much suspicion.

In Valley of Winds marriages had taken place only within Father's clan, and by then there were only a handful of people who were not deformed. Most of the children died before they reached the age of three, and I had no paternal cousins. Father himself had lost most of his hearing.

The clan, which had more than thirty members, went on living in small clusters, each consisting of several, to the east and the west of the land they owned. The earthen storehouse given to Father and me was at the northern end where a cedar wood began immediately behind it. The odors of hay and chickens drifted in the air wherever you went. The diluted sun that managed to come through Valley of Winds would pass by the tiny window of the store-house in a moment, and the night would come before you had time to bat an eye. The emaciated moon would pass along like a prolonged exhaling, taking its time.

I was carried into the storehouse in a coma and never met anyone in Valley of Winds. For the brief period before Japan was defeated and we left, I met only people like the moonlight, a stew with a lot of pumpkin in it, and the sound of a bucket in the well.

At the same time I was friendly with everyone in Valley of Winds. Even now, several decades later, if I were to meet them in the distant world, I'd never mistake them. I even knew the habit of my grandmother, already dead then, who never failed to start cooking cabbage late at night, at eleven o'clock. I was also friendly with the people who appeared on the walls or the floor of the storehouse, who were half like human beings, half like smoke.

In the darkness they would show their tongues and fingers as they intently chattered away. And before you knew it, they would be lying on the desk, in the forms of pencils and spoons.

—*Valley of Winds*

It's difficult to tell you about Valley of Winds. I try to concentrate and gaze at it, but I can't accurately depict that gray mansion in my thoughts.

Winds were always singing in the sky, over the cliff, all around.

The fragrance of death pervaded the air.

Mixed with the fragrance of summer grass, it drifted like smoke as far as the bar in the stable and the well. Also, a mysterious being called Okiki-san inhabited the dark of the house, appearing and disappearing, playing small pranks. But neither the gray windows nor the gray entrance come into focus to make clear images. The moment I give up all—the way those things were there, the thought of telling you about them, the effort to remember them—

I don't know why, but they are there, nonchalantly.

The horses in their stable,
the cricket on the bar,
Okiki-san in the dark of the oven.

—*The Storehouse*

What was given to the father and the child was the second floor of the earthen storehouse. It had only two small windows, and through them the light from outside shone in, making patches each the size of a newspaper, as the mornings and nights passed.

Father spent half of every day by the well, washing my nightie that was heavy with sweat. The creaking noise of the well-bucket, along with the sound of the winds, filled the semi-darkness of the storehouse. The sweat increased night after night. There was no drug, no means to lower my fever.

In the evening an iron pot seemed to be delivered from the main house. A stew with a small amount of rice and pumpkin cooked into it. That was a day's worth of meal for us. Father would accept the iron pot prayerfully and put it below a small window. In that meager light the meal was finished swiftly.

The light from the window became smaller even while we watched. The last drop of the light swayed like a dream on the yellow of the pumpkin, and in no time it was deep into night.

—Rabbit's Story

Look. That's the storehouse where you and your father live. In the old days it had stacks of brass braziers and boxes in it. They were all given up for the war effort. They may have turned into guns and things somewhere. Now the second floor has the two of you, and below, it's full of hay and mulberry leaves, you see.

The detached quarter to the east is where your youngest aunt lies in bed. She's been sick, for a long time now. She mayn't last until August.

Your grandmother is sleeping with her daughter—

So that *she* may call someone when her suffering begins. Not your blood-related grandmother. Your real grandmother is asleep in the ground on the hill at back. She died very long ago, right after giving birth to your father.

And that is the main house. A surprise, isn't it, a whole group of thirty uncles and aunts and cousins are living there. In the attics are silkworms asleep. A large loom, too; and two horses in the stable. There by the oven where a stew with pumpkin is being cooked, you see Okiki-san. The same Okiki-san like gray smoke.

In the evening it began to rain.

Okiki-san wove in the attic all night long.

The big family slept listening to the clank-clank sound in their dreams. It was at such a time that bad news was quietly stepping toward Valley of Winds.

—The Staircases

In that old summer, the second floor of the storehouse where I lay ill had two almost identical holes, made side by side on the floor boards, through which you went down. Both ladders were steep. Toward their bottoms something like light mist drifted, with occasional faint odors of mulberry leaves.

"Make sure not to climb down the staircase to the nether world," Father said the night we reached the storehouse. That was the summer when we came to his home town to escape the air raids. His home town was overflowing with relatives and relations who had become victims of war. The only living quarter left for my father and me was the storehouse.

"Your grandmother used to say, 'This storehouse has an entrance to the nether world.' She'd say that whenever she put a naughty boy in here." Sitting cross-legged across the entrance invisible to him, and relieved, Father was intent on telling the old stories he remembered.

"Let's go," an uncle said. He was in a boy-soldier's uniform. He had been killed in battle in the depths of Manchuria, but was now standing at the entrance.

"Let's go," an infant aunt said. She'd been laid up for a long time with tuberculosis in a six-mat room away from the main quarters. She died in August, at daybreak. "Let's go," she said. She cackled with laughter and, laughing, kept enlarging her mouth. The darkness of her throat, as it was, expanded on the floor and turned into the entrance to the depths below. The odor of mulberry leaves, along with the morning, filled the air. Following Uncle and Aunt I was ready to climb down the ladder. Uncle's shoulders tilted and were about to fade in the mist. Aunt's white hands were busily trying to put a pair of straw sandals on me. For this village had the custom of having a dead person wear straw sandals. But all the pairs were too large for me. There were also sandals that were as small as flower petals.

Aunt dropped away into the mist to buy a more fitting pair of sandals.

And she never returned.

—The Coffin on the Moonlit Night

On moonlit nights they were especially busy.
Stepping on pearlworts, crossing the river,
Aunt and others with their white hands would come.
They formed a circle in the yard to the east.
They chatted among themselves like reeds.

On moonlit nights the job of the aunt and others was to make boxes.
The yard would fill with the noises of saws cutting cedar boards.
40 centimeters, 60 centimeters, 180 centimeters.
Hurry, hurry, Aunt and others whispered among themselves.
Before the moon goes away, you see.
40 centimeters, 60 centimeters, hurry, please.
It was very hard to make square boxes with any accuracy in the moonlight.
The white hands of Aunt and others, fifty to sixty of them, would sough as they swayed like pampas grass.
The moon, round and disfigured, was walking toward the cedar wood.

In the midst of the yard, boxes lay hazy as dreams.
Nails, please, one said; Wait, another one said.
Listen, isn't 180 centimeters too long?
It isn't, the person in the detached quarter is tall, you know.
Oh, I thought, someone in the distance said.
—I thought this box was for the child lying in the storehouse.
Aunt and others held the nails in their mouths, soughing, swaying,
as the moon, turned into a tiny face, floated beyond the wood.

About the box in the moonlit night, it's also difficult to tell you accurately.

It was like the other moon shining in the moonlight,
as in a pool of water.
As the nails were hammered in, the box swayed, turned gray,
acquiring in no time the hue of the ground.
Aunt and others swayed, acquiring the hue of the ground, saying,
Hurry, hurry.
As the moon rose,
I've been running, all night, toward the box,
but still can't get there.
That's why I still can't tell you
the story inside the box.

—Travels on Moonlit Nights

As the moon rose every night I had to go out to travel. No drug or injection could bring me back from my travels. The shoes for traveling were as hot as fire. The bag for traveling stuck to my back like a fireball. Along with the shadowy Rabbit I went out on my hot, bitter travels.

Small Aunt was eighteen years old and was in the terminal stage of pulmonary tuberculosis. She was asleep in a room to the east. As Rabbit and I crossed the yard, the light from her room, turned into a disfigured square, lay on the ground. And every night it would float up from the depths of the earth as it took the shape of a large coffin.

—The Small Aunt

Let's go together," small Aunt said.
She was in a sailor suit as she sat near my pillow.
Her hair mistily drifted throughout the room.
"Let's go," her distant voice said.
I'd feel lonesome if I went alone.
It's dark beyond Valley of Winds.

—Somewhere the 7 o'clock news had begun.
Bulletin from the Eastern Seaboard Military District HQ: *For about two and a half hours last night, approximately 70 B-29's bombed residential quarters of the city.*

The next night Aunt stared at me from the high window of the
storehouse.
"Let's go," she said.
Through her large black eyes, mist flowed down, down.
"I'm lonesome.
I'll lend you my lace boots, you know."

The third night
Aunt stood there with Mother's face.
"Let's go back to Tokyo," she said.
I shook my head violently.
Aunt was struggling hard
to make a smiling face exactly like Mother's.
Her face began to collapse from her mouth,
then scattered away into styptic grass.

—The news had begun.
. . . As a result of the air raids fires broke out, but they were mostly brought under control by daybreak.

Some nights later
Aunt lay in a box in the yard.
Smiling a little.
Mist thinly moved around the box.
"Put on the lid now," she said.
"The lid is in the cedar wood."
I began walking toward the cedar wood.

The wood seemed to grow gradually distant.
Both hands and feet felt heavy, hot,
and at every step I seemed to sink into the ground.
. . . Damages on our strategic facilities have been exceedingly slight.
Bulletin from Western Military District HQ.
Whose voice was it?
I turned back, and the box
had already become vague, vague,
now ready to fade away.
'Cause I'll be lonesome, said Aunt from the bottom of the box.

I returned from my dark travels.
I took off my red shoes.
Aunt is dead, I told Father.

—Dark Valley

Small Aunt had begun to rot. What shall I do? Her coffin wasn't ready in time. Not a single person in Valley of Winds could procure boards and nails. Aunt and others with white hands who rose up from the depths of the earth every night had grown bored of coffin-making long before. All they did was to swarm all over the yard like pampas grass and sing to themselves vainly, restlessly.

—Go to Dark Valley to dump it.
Dark Valley is a nice place.

Small Aunt had begun to rot. What shall I do? The day of Japan's defeat was just around the corner. No one knew it. Everybody just walked around the corpse. There were no boards or nails. What shall I do? Only the golden hair of the sun in its abundance kept turning round Valley of Winds.

The small coffin for me was carried out of the storehouse. Someone thought of putting Aunt in it. It was a coffin Father had made for me by taking apart an orange crate—such an awful thing that today even a cat would hesitate to lie in it. Even now, when I'm past forty, I can remember the box accurately. On the day of my death I'd like at least my heart to be put in it. It's something Father made, bloodying his fingers. It's the essence of the clumsy mind of the one I loved the most.

The coffin was too small for small Aunt. What shall I do? They bent her legs, twisted her neck, but still couldn't lay her in it. The moon rose. What shall I do now? White hands crawled out of the earth in countless numbers and Aunt and others began to make merry.

—Cut off her legs, cut off her arms.

—Go to Dark Valley, after cutting off her legs, cutting off her arms.

Firewood was piled up on a carriage. Aunt wrapped in a sheet was placed on it. Father pulling the cart, the whole clan walked to Dark Valley. In that region, the custom required that the corpses of those who died of infectious diseases be burnt in Dark Valley, cattle and pigs included. Aunt and others with white hands rising up from the bottom of the night gradually increased in number as they drifted like mist around the cart. When we passed a schoolhouse, its bulletin board had the latest war news pasted on it. The village had few radios, so everyone read it in the moonlight in hushed voices.

—*In the said attack the enemy appears to have used a new type of bomb. . . .*

After that we all fell silent and, hand in hand, went down to Dark Valley. Small Aunt herself went down alone, with her quiet footfall, into an even deeper darkness.

Every night we ate a light stew with leaves of sweet potato in it. Every night small Aunt came with the moon. In a sailor suit, looking down, she would slowly walk toward the schoolhouse. The whole family would stop moving their chopsticks, looking at her as she walked away. Since she no longer had a body, skinny rabbits, skinny frogs, bats, winged insects, and other late-night things swam through her, toward the western sky. About that time the moonlit nights began to show a faint suggestion of rotting.

—The Mud House

In the marshland skunk cabbages were at their peak.
A silvery stream was purling through it.
Father was washing a horse.
He was to travel to the village of Kirio;
was to go through a wood
and cross a field of umbrella plants.
In a very small voice I called, "Father."
When Father turned, I said in an even smaller voice, "Listen."
"Listen, are you going to Kirio, Father?"
"I am. Since morning you've asked that same question ten times."
All over the sky
the sun was untangling its golden hair.
"Do you want something from Kirio?"
I hastily shook my head.
"I want nothing. I just thought that Gorō might be back from Tokyo."
One skunk cabbage
was faintly red
as if a sudden light had turned on.
Father was to travel.
A bright short trip.
"All right, I'll give him your regards."
It was when skunk cabbages were at their peak.
Father and summer grew small across the field.

If I had such a day of love while I was a girl—
I was sleeping as I continued that thought.
Deep in the mud house I was ill for months.
Infantile tuberculosis was gradually destroying me.
The war was destroying the nation from one end to the other.
With the odors of bombs and hunger the mud house was about to
collapse.

Splattered with mud I was drifting through the marshland.
Aunt and others in the distant world
had stretched countless numbers of white hands to the end of the
marshland.
"Come, darling,
come over here."
They called to me night and day.
"The bottom of the mud is quiet.
Come over here."
The war-fires spread
and the nation was about to collapse.
Only the sun was letting its abundant golden hair
flow all over the sky.
Father did not return from his trip.
As I fell toward the bottom of the mud, I uttered a faint cry,
said to no one in particular, "Gorō."
I also tried, "Good night."

—The Imperative Form

My, did you shrink?
(Wearing an air raid hood.)

At times I remember the bulletin board in the small village. Often it stands erect in my dreams. It's of a very ordinary sort, painted, that you see at the entrance, for example, of a gathering place for old people.

In the village called Valley of Winds where I evacuated during the war, that bulletin board was close to being the only source of information. The arrangement was that the news heard on the radio at the mayor's house was written on a sheet of paper, which was then pasted on the board.

In that village evening came early, and the people who had finished working in the fields would gather at the schoolhouse and read the daily news. My granduncle, who could read, read the news aloud, repeatedly. Most of the information had to do with the war situation, plus the damage from air raids.

—Our damages were negligible. All the fires were brought under control by daybreak—

Granduncle's voice would spread through the evening darkness and the village would sink into the night. Generally the way days passed like that.

Near Japan's defeat, one evening the news item was fairly long.

—On August 6, Hiroshima City sustained considerable damage. The enemy appears to have used a new type of bomb in the said attack, but the details are unknown. Enemy though he is, he must have developed a splendid weapon…

Voiceless, everyone went home. We cooked a watery stew with leaves of sweet potato. We cracked an egg and dropped it into it. The night was almost lacquer black; at times a stray firefly or two flew past, dragging their tails.

(My, you're back again.
The war came to an end long ago, you know.)

In the dream, as I come to that steep path, I am as soon and unmistakably out at the schoolhouse. It's very sad. In the moonlight we read the news in a chorus. Together with the skinny rabbit and granduncle long gone.

Give them words.
Plant pumpkins.

The windows of Broom Store (seems like a house name),
turn off the lights,
turn off the lights of wasteland chamomiles.

Throw beans at enemy planes.
Throw dogs into the pots, pluck rabbits.

In a chorus we read the news. Rabbit, surprised a little, was touching his ears. All of us were soughing like pampas grass in the deep night.

(My, you are still here.
Valley of Winds has ceased to be, you know.)

Watch out everywhere, east, west, south, north.
Hear nothing, go to the hole.

Don't turn back to look.
Don't let your bugle go. Smile at death.

Without your arms and legs,
it's peace: nether world.

On a wooden chair in the schoolhouse I was having a lesson. The students resembled rabbits or clouds. Somewhere at a great distance a siren had begun to sound.
My, you still have page five open?
In a clear, high-pitched voice the teacher said.
We're finished with our study of the imperative form.

—The Wind Seller

At one end of Valley of Winds a small man who sold winds had arrived. August, the onset of autumn. It's a little too early, but I have autumnal winds to sell. He was calling out. With a scythe he would swiftly slice a wind out of the air, stuff it into a paper bag, and hand it to the villagers.

The wind upstream of the Janome River is a good *thing* for a special occasion, he said. He had spent three days to get to the source of the river.

On days when the water level rose, the sound of the waves of the river reached me as I slept in the depths of the storehouse.

"You say winds of high quality, but what are they?"

Deep in my deep sleep, I once asked him.

"Well, they are the ones mixed with dragonflies and leaves and things. Of course, these come *free*, and you don't have to pay for them."

"Then what's poor quality?"

"Well, the ones from Dark Valley don't sell."

"They don't come mixed with dragonflies. . . ?"

"Nahhh," he hastily waved his hand. The air around us, on a day when autumn was near, filled with the fragrances of nuts and fire.

The ones with nothing mixed in them are, by themselves, of high quality, he said. "The ones there have hands and webs thrown in them and aren't any good."

He picked up one of the heavy-looking paper bags. The villagers burned a variety of things in Dark Valley: horses struck down by plague, a great many chickens and ducks in the year the epidemic called *oro'oro* struck. My aunt who died of pulmonary tuberculosis was also cremated at the bottom of the valley.

Amused perhaps by the way I stepped backward, he laughed with a hooting voice like an engine whistle. He grew larger with his voice. His head bulged out of the forest and seemed to turn into a cloud, beginning with the tip of his hands. I watched his palms that had already turned almost into clouds stuff one of the distant clouds into a bag. In this way the village was to avalanche into an early autumn.

—*August 15, 1945*

Late at night Father came back to the room in the storehouse. In those days his job, from morning to night, was to catch frogs in the swamp to add to the food for the whole clan. We cooked those small white fragments of flesh with sweet-potato leaves and ate them.

"Tomorrow at twelve, I'll be going to the mayor's house," Father said, near my pillow. The village had few radios with good reception. The custom therefore was for the villagers to gather at the mayor's house in order to listen to important broadcasts.

"They say there's going to be a very, very important talk, from His Majesty," Father said to me in a voice so low it was almost inaudible, as he wiped sweat off my brow.

"We're losing the war."

August 15. My fever was high. After Father left for the mayor's house, the darkness of the storehouse filled with mysterious beings: Okiki-san, my small Aunt, my great-grandfather who had only one arm. The small man who sold winds made me hold a pinch of autumn wind. Everyone sang in unison, "Good night, good night." That was the end of the war that I, still young, faced.

—*Summer 1950*

We were cooking apricots. Both the dining room and the corridor were filled with their sweet smell. The telephone at the end of the corridor rang. Mother ran to it. The corridor was so bright as to be blinding, and on the lawn a girl's laughter was ringing. In the middle of the corridor, in the brightness of the sun, I suddenly saw Rabbit. My scream and Mother's voice of alarm overlapped. Holding the receiver, Mother held her paled face turned toward me. I thought I was pointing at Rabbit who was there, but he had disappeared into the darkness of the inner room.

"... For the first time in five years," my voice, at once an attempt to hide my embarrassment and an excuse, again overlapped with Mother's voice.

"Shōgo—his bones found—on Mount Amagi—," she said.

Shōgo was the name of Mother's younger brother, the only one among my maternal uncles that I met while they were alive.

Mother and I took care of Uncle's funeral. Several more years later, it came to light that he had two children. We heard from somewhere that one of the children had visited one of Mother's distant relatives.

I ended up asking neither the child's gender nor the region of his residence. At the time I felt that those children were the human beings remotest from me in this world. I will not run into them in the future either.

As for Uncle Shōgo, even now I run into him from time to time. He may be seated in front of the lottery during a retailers' festival or on a train late at night. Wearing leggings and the shoes he had stolen from Father who was in dire poverty, he always looks distracted. Not because he's pretending out of embarrassment, but because he truly doesn't know me, it seems, he doesn't recognize me.

He had too many painful experiences, so "Forgive him everything," Rabbit said. You see, there aren't many things that are so bad you can't forgive. This uncle, who put all the relatives in difficult straits and forced them to disperse, took poison in the depths of Mount Amagi, so that he might forget everything, and in the hope that he might be forgotten by everyone. In the dark of the nether world he continued to drink from the spring of forgetfulness. And he was distracted, Rabbit said.

Except there's one thing he shouldn't forget, Uncle thought from time to time in an abstract sort of way. The names of the two small, very small children—thinking to try to remember them, Uncle sways on the train of night.

—*The Shoes*

If you turn the corner at the *hampen* store, you see that semi-dark shoe shop. On such a night the town is suffocating with the old odors of August. As if in a set scene, the white-haired shop owner emerges, intently looking along the street.

I open the terribly old wooden door. It creaks, making a horrible noise. Tin-like things, web-like things, fill the shop, it gets heavier and darker toward the back. You cross a swampy thing to go further inside. On the highest display shelf are those shoes.

They have no price tag, and are made almost of mud. In the dark near the ceiling, it's a mystery that you can tell they are shoes.

—They're the shoes his corpse wore.

From behind me the shop owner speaks to me.

—I know. These are my father's shoes.

I would respond with a bluntest voice.

—You mean, the person who committed suicide on Mount Amagi was your father?

—No, he wasn't. Far from it. He was Mother's youngest brother and he had stolen my father's shoes. He was a crook, and someone was always after him. Probably he was wearing my father's shoes, if anything, on the day he died.

—How can you tell they were his?

—I can tell wherever I see them. They always have a faint light entangled in them. Besides, they carry the odors of that August. Don't they have our old address written inside? They were the only shoes of my father, and I remember him carefully writing his name with ink.

—The uncle. . . .

—Please don't ask me about the uncle. I have nothing to do with my maternal relations.

—You mean you hate your mother and her brothers.

He would ask with a hooting voice that was like an engine whistle in the distance.

—I wish I could hate them. Hatred has the power to bring people together. Mine is *indifference*. Even on the day when I pass through the darkness of the nether world I am unlikely to run into my uncle.

The shop owner was now standing by the display shelves. Holding the mud-like shoes against the moonlight, he was trying to read the distant address. The siren had begun to sound. An air raid. In the four directions of the town, fires rose up, and the sky and the ground were shaking in one big scream. The shoes became smaller and smaller, lying quietly in the dark light on the night uncle came to deceive my father.

—*August*

In the shoes I can see Father wearily walking a sodden road. He was barefooted. The old August. The air was full of the odors of miscanthus and muddy swamp. He was carrying a tin bucket, an insect net on his shoulder.

The swamp was in season for frogs. Father was intently scooping up frogs and skinning them. The frogs were smoothly peeled from their mouths. That August, the only things that were abundant in a meager village called Valley of Winds where we had evacuated were frogs, locusts, and the glittering golden hair that the sun untangled.

Father's hands were immediately dyed with blood, and because of its sliminess frogs easily slipped out of his palms. One or two of them slid into the swamp after they were skinned.

They flutter as they swim toward the bottom of the shoes. No matter how deeply I close my eyes, I can see their white bodies.

I drag the swampy shoes as I traverse the days and months, days and months, from village to town; that's what I am.

—*The Grandfather*

On the day of Aunt's funeral I saw the owner of that shoe shop.

In Aunt's old album he was standing, modestly looking down, with everything that surrounded him already turned reddish brown, neither the background nor the appearance of his suit clearly definable.

"Who is this?" I asked one of my cousins who had returned to the living room.

"My." She stared at me as if surprised. "He's grandfather," she said.

"Grandfather . . . mine?"

"Yes, ours . . . you see. He's the one who was in Kamata and was killed in an air raid." Her beautiful eyes wide open, she stared at me as if in disbelief.

—So that's who you were, Grandfather. Even more surprised than my cousin, I was gazing at the owner of the shoe shop.

—Grandfather. Every night, I neglected to say hello to you, but late on such lonesome nights you were dealing in shoes in a town like that that no one went to visit. Whenever I wandered into that town, you displayed my father's shoes, didn't you? Did you mean to return to me his shoes that your youngest son had stolen?

Grandfather. In the *hampen* store, red and white *hampen* were about to be made. A great many plum-blossom-shaped *hampen* were being lined up on the cooking board.

My cousin surprised me further with her clear, high-pitched voice.

"That's right. The *hampen* store!" she said.

"You knew, didn't you? Our grandfather died in the air raid shelter of the *hampen* maker. It was in May, and there were those air raids following the 'frying pan' tactic. . . ."

"What's 'frying pan'?"

My cousin looked a little lost and hesitated.

"You see, first they would spray oil from the sky. Then they would drop incendiary bombs in such a way as to encircle the town. The people inside had no way of escaping and would burn to death. That was the tactic. Our grandfather died in one of those raids. I went in the old abandoned underground water main at the back of the shrine and when I came out I found myself on the riverbed."

—The Starry Moonlit Night

The moon rose and Valley of Winds sank into a whitish light. Father and his clan shuffled together in the yard to the east.

Fire was kindled in a large oven. On an iron sheet valuable oil was poured and sweet-potato leaves and frogs were thrown on it.

Father was washing his bloody hands. When he removed a pebble that had pressed into his sole, light blood oozed out of that spot as well.

The moonlight was falling on the well and the bucket.

On the iron sheet frogs shrank quickly.

Surrounding the fire Uncles and Aunt were plying their chopsticks.

The small fragments of flesh, along with the moonlight, disappeared into their dark mouths.

They were soft and sweet, like a certain kind of river fish.

The August of Valley of Winds filled with the odors of frog and fire. The stars that had begun to increase near the moon now infested the whole sky. But I could no longer make out the constellation Cowherd or the constellation Hair. One of the large stars suddenly ballooned, became disfigured, and began crumbling down onto my chest wasted by illness.

—*The Electric Calculator*

I must be with her till her last moments—Father said. It was at the ladder from the second floor of the storehouse to the entrance. I thought my end had finally come.

Since my small Aunt died—yes, on August 6, the day an atomic bomb was dropped, she died. It was pulmonary tuberculosis. She spewed out all her lung organisms before dying, everybody said. I didn't see it. Her screams of pain traveled from the *detached* room where she was, to my storehouse, though. But all that soon ended.

Deep sleep came to capture me. The night and the moon came together. After Aunt, it was my turn. Everyone was waiting for it. A line-up like that rarely goes out of whack, you know.

With what kind of face is Death going to come visit me, so wondering, I waited intently with my eyes open, even in my sleep. I'd rather that Death be that Rabbit, I thought. It was supposed to come up that unreliable ladder.

"You mean your father came to see you die?"

No, my father went to see the last moments of that old electric calculator.

"What do you mean by the last moments of a calculator?"

You see, it was used to help the work of the Navy Ministry. With such a thing lying about, the American soldiers are sure to kill us, my grandfather and uncles were afraid. Late at night, the surviving members of the clan dug a hole in the backyard. It was a very deep hole. The calculator was tied with ropes and sank into the darkness of the hole. My father covered it with soil. The uncles were stamping the soil with their feet. I could sense the moon's loud derisive laughter gradually disappearing into the west. The clan, soaked pale blue, were secretively circling over the hole.

—*Questions & Answers*

Late on misty nights I was often questioned in the court. The questions were simple. And my answers were clear. But the questioner was uncertain every night, and the reasons for questioning me were even more unclear.

—That was the last night my father was a mathematician. I answered. My voice bounced back from the invisible wall and poisonously returned near my chest. I tried to look away from the judgment I myself spat out, but at once it sank to the bottom of my stomach like mud and congealed in some place I could not reach.

"Well then, the calculator is still buried in the ground of Valley of Winds, isn't it?"

No, it doesn't seem to be.

"What do you mean?"

I don't remember when, but I met him. It was evening. A dark man was walking the road that runs along the embankment where the English conversation school is. He was a very small man. In the diluted evening sun he looked as if he was made of mud.

"You are saying that was the calculator."

Yes.

"You often meet strange things like Rabbit of the nether world and lost shoes."

Yes, I am born to notice such things instantly.

"So, what did he do?"

He went down toward the river and out of sight. When I returned home, I found a notice from Grandmother (here, what I mean is Father's stepmother). It said that the calculator was exhibited in "Life During the War," that someone bought it for a high price, that she, the grandmother, accepted the money in lieu of our rent for the storehouse in Valley of Winds. Well, it went something like that.

"You mean they bothered to dig it up."

Yes, Grandmother liked anything that attracted attention. Besides, by then you didn't have to worry that American soldiers might kill you. Rather, the general idea was taking hold that as long as you had collaborated in the war, it would be more gallant to step forward and make the confession before anybody said anything about it. Even if things turned out badly, Grandmother wouldn't have been damaged in any way. Besides, she liked money more than anything else. I myself wouldn't say I dislike money, that would be silly, but ever since I came to know her, I've seldom met anyone who likes money as much as she did.

"You're laughing. Whenever you touch this subject, you never fail to laugh. Are you aware of that?"

The laughing is for myself. I am sorry. This is the way it has been since the summer the war ended.

Even after they buried the calculator, the clan was worried. A strange song made a round of Valley of Winds as people whispered.

The spring is dark.
Americans are coming.
Nether flowers are dark.
Japanese will be killed.

Grandmother told us to leave before the people of the valley saw us. Father and I prepared to travel.

"You were nearly dying of an illness, weren't you?"

I was put on a cart. September was close and it was night. We went by the valley road, relying on the light from the river. I was laughing by myself. We could see nothing. The night grew deeper, and there was only the sound of the river. Unable to walk another step, Father fell with a thud into something like pampas grass. Without uttering a sound, I was laughing my lone laugh. To fall asleep all by yourself, that is the most fitting thing.

—*Sleeping Under the Open Sky*

We left Valley of Winds behind us the year we lost the war, when August was about to end. Father put me on a cart and left our home in his home town where that earthen storehouse was. There were few things to carry, and the cart was weighed down only by me and a blanket. Perhaps this was something we could count as luck.

Father walked as much as he was able to walk, and late at night he dropped straight into pampas grass and slept. Sleeping under the open sky. Falling asleep, he said faintly, "Must be a *gorosuke hō*." Was an owl hooting? Or was the night so quiet that even my near-deaf father could hear an owl? I slept, simply listening to the loud voice of the night. The voice was so extravagantly loud that it could not pull me out of my sleep.

—*Father's Résumé*

I am often asked the reason Father left Valley of Winds, taking a sick child with him, without any place to go to. Well, the reason was simple. During the war, he was commissioned by the Ministry of the Navy to compute "differential equations for ballistic calculations." His clan's worry was that if this was known to the American side, they might be killed. They buried the old calculator in a hole. They chased Father and me out. Even then, they busied themselves thinking up excuses just in case American soldiers came. Of course, no American or British soldiers came. Some years later, Father wrote a series entitled "My Résumé" for an economic daily; according to his account there, the "ballistic calculations" served no purpose. When the calculations were completed, the Empire of Japan had long run out of rockets to be used. Father, who loved Japan dearly, couldn't speak of the pitiful state of his country for a long time.

To me, who doesn't truly love Japan, or any other country, or anything else, things like rockets are of no concern. But I fear one thing: that in "My Résumé" there isn't a single reference to Valley of Winds, to my illness, or to his clan.

Are they—Valley of Winds, my small Aunt, the calculator buried deep in the ground—simply among those who have appeared only on the road of my nightmares through which I am passing? "My Résumé" has just one line concerning me—saying, My daughter was born in May 1935.

—Night Dew

Throughout the night, those people came in and out of my sleep. My small Aunt, whom I had never had a chance to meet in life, walked into my sleep with special vividness. I could even see clearly the school insignia, a lily, sewn into the collar of her sailor suit. She sat on the grass by the river and asked, "Are you going home?"

You'll never come back here again, I know it—she said. Then suddenly she became invisible, with only her large eyes remaining. "I don't like you," the eyes said.

—You're always with a strange rabbit. But he looks very old, and besides, he isn't good-looking at all.

Okiki-san was busy preparing for a trip.

I'm going to Fujishiro's house down stream, she said.

On the night someone died, she never failed to weave in the attic.

That was a custom in Valley of Winds.

"For a while I won't be coming to your house," she said. —Everyone who was to die has died, you know, in your place. Another thing—she said as she filled her water bottle with the water from the bucket.

"I won't see you any more.

"You won't come back here again."

Before you knew it, Okiki-san had grown small, and pasted herself flat in a corner of a picture book as if she were an illustration. The bucket remained tilted, and the water kept pouring out, its splashes making me wet like night dew.

Two nights sleeping under the open sky. We ate dried sweet potato by the river. We saw a flotilla of ducks crossing the river. Father was chasing fish in the river in the morning glow. Were they dace? If we ran out of the meager amount of sweet potato that an uncle had put in the chest space of my kimono when grandmother wasn't looking, we'd exhaust our food. But no fish was dumb enough to be caught by Father with his bare hands, and he returned to me, soaking wet. When we passed Dark Valley, I heard the voice of the wind seller, which had grown completely hoarse soughing over the treetops, saying, "This is a wind especially set aside for you." "A wind with dragonfly wings, all free." Where the voice suddenly ceased was where Valley of Winds ended. It was another region, another village, whose name I no longer could remember. It was dazzling flat country.

—*The Yard*

In the yard of a farmhouse, Father had put the cart he was pulling with me on it. He seemed to have requested water. The young wife of the house ran to me. She must have been startled by my wasted appearance.

How old are you? she asked.

"Fourth grade in national school."

I replied with a voice horrifying and cracked as if it had arisen from the depths of the earth. Then suddenly I realized that I hadn't heard my own voice for a long time.

The wife quickly cut open my pillow. The husks that stuffed it spilled to the ground and stirred up a small swirl of dust in the evening sun.

After coming back from the inside of the house, she was tightly sewing up the pillow in which she had stuffed rice. Perhaps she wanted to keep it a secret from her family. Moving her needle in terrible haste, she pricked her coarse fingers several times.

"This may help a little," she said. Then she made me hold the pillow and slowly tried to make herself understood.

"Treasure this, all right? Don't just cook it and eat it, no, miss. You put it in a soup and cook it. Slowly, slowly, on a slow fire. Put leaves and potatoes in it, too."

My memory of the yard ends there. A single tree at the end of the yard. Its emaciated red flowers go on sinking into the semi-darkness, and somewhere at a great distance an infant's voice is saying, "Thank you, thank you very much." —Slowly, over a slow fire. So repeats the young farmer, farther into the darkness.

It must have been soon after the shrine festival. In the roadside shrine there was a candle left burning. Under its small light we spent the night. Beyond the shrine spread a wild-looking field of reeds, and at its end the evening glow turned dark even while you watched. Water and the last bit of dried sweet potato made up our night meal. "Ōshima. . .that was it."

Staring at the candle, Father suddenly mumbled; it must have been the family name of the farmer who had helped us earlier. The night swiftly filled the shrine hall. The darkness spread its brown arms and swayed on the earthen walls.

"Cook. Well. On a slow fire," Father repeated.

"See, it's a square root. Some nights back, I taught you this.

"It's the square root of six: 2.449489.†

"You always—since you were very small,

"You would ask me about the numbers that don't exist in this world—"

I was about to fall asleep. I seem to remember I was shaking my head persistently.

—Something more important—somebody had said. I'd had enough of mathematical talk.

Square roots, what in the world are they!

At the entrance to sleep, there was a very white, infant rabbit. He was dipping his hands in the field stream, intently washing wooden shoes. Before you knew it, the wooden shoes were full of gold coins.

One of the gold coins flowed into my hands and uttered a sudden laugh.

"It's *crepe myrtle*, they say."

† As a mnemonic device, Japanese sometimes read certain numerals in such a way as to make sense as statements. In this instance, the square root of six is read to mean "cook well over a slow fire."

Far away from me looking puzzled, Rabbit said. Whether it was Father's voice or Rabbit's, I no longer could tell. Still, in a sleep that gradually became deeper, I continued to think: some day, in the future, I would also say with all my heart to a small child: Slowly. Over a slow fire. How old are you? Where are you from? Where are you going, all by yourself? Are you going to see the setting sun? Slowly, very slowly, be careful . . . you see.

—*Interlude*

Whenever a yellowish night came, your court would seem to convene. You would question me endlessly. The following is a small fraction of the records.

"Yesterday I perused the documents related to your father. He was a mathematician, wasn't he? The Iwanami edition of the *Encyclopedia of Mathematics* had some entry on him. Is he still active as a mathematician?"

No, it's perhaps a little different. I'm afraid this is a very unclear way to put it. Several years after the war ended, he moved into the business world. You might say he succeeded. Our living conditions seem to have improved. As my father's work began to attract attention, my mother came back.

"You mean from her lover's place."

Probably yes.

"Did you hate your mother?"

No, not at all. I never had any interest in my mother as a human being. To me, my mother was utter nonsense. When it comes to her lover, he has less meaning than a shadow.

"After your living conditions improved, what was your home like?"

I have no accurate knowledge of my house since about that time. Beginning around 1950 it gradually became impossible for me to belong to my home, my family. My father, mother, sister, all quickly began to recede into the distance. In the end, my family, my house, even the town where we lived, turned into something like an image of a magic lantern cast in the darkness.

The only thing I did was, on rare occasion, I'd be terrified by too much solitude and call out the name of my father or sister.

"What did your family do when that happened?"

They appeared to grow smaller, more distant than ever.

"But you still took your meals with them, lived with them while going to school, didn't you?"

It seems I did.

"Was your family cold to you?"

No, they were very nice—I think they were. My father had turned into a man who looked dignified and stately to everyone. My mother became more beautiful than ever. But I can't grasp very well the phenomena flowing over such surfaces. My "real father" was always in that shipwrecked two-storied house. He still is. He's solving mathematical formulas. It may be his work for the Ministry of the Navy. That old-fashioned electric calculator is on. I can see the westerly sun of the late summer pouring into the room like a flood.

Between breaks in his work my father is teaching me mathematics. I see straw-sheets with mathematical formulas written on them scattered here and there in the room.

"I take it you suffered from terrible malnutrition in those days."

Yes, I had a high fever for days on end. On such nights, Rabbit never failed to show up. In the dark of the wall, first his paws would stick out. Then his eyes. then his grass-blade-like ears. He would say, "Come with me."

"You would go out with the rabbit. You would go through a number of narrow, dark holes. When you were almost out of breath, you would reach that room. Do you remember that room?"

I spent almost all nights in that room. There, Rabbit looked like a thin tin plate. A chair and a large tin pot. That old woman, who always showed up, would pour something like soup for me. "Eat it, please eat it," she would say. Her voice was like water or rain. The soup was forever poured into the crack at my feet and never filled my plate.

My life appeared short. My father was calling my name in a ripping voice.

"Then?"

If I ever meet you once again, I will tell you what happened afterwards. If possible, please go visit that two-storied house, too. Rabbit's giant shadow is still walking in the house.

—*The House*

No one now remembers where the house was, what it looked like. We see it only when we take a walk inside the memory of that girl wasted to skin and bone. Today, just finding the girl, who was in grade school when the war ended, is extremely difficult. From time to time she appears at the end of the field and is saying something in a hoarse voice. Our ears that have grown less sensitive over the years have difficulty capturing that voice.

What stands palely at the end of summer grass and rubble is that house.

The land about 500 square feet. A triangular lot. The house was built on a disfigured square

For its small size, its entrance was so enormous as to look silly. Often there were frogs on the concrete floor. The second floor looking ready to fall down. To the west, in a triangular room, I was always asleep.

Still dazed by the shock of the air raid, the house stood precariously. For a long time it looked as if it couldn't believe the miracle of having escaped the fire.

"Everything is over."

On the day we returned from Valley of Winds, I told that to the house many times. The house, however, merely looked at me with suspicion, as it vainly stretched its *soot-colored* arm toward the falling sun.

September of that year. Evening darknesses came into the house more swiftly than they had in any other year. They invaded it through the cracked glass windows, through the spaces around the door, one after another, calling to the next group, "Hurry, hurry!"

They would disperse to the bathtub, to the kitchen floor, in quick steps, and begin to sing among themselves in a low, soughing voices.

"You all, we all."

Distraction and Ravage would begin to emerge from the shutter box and from under the floor. They held a small child born between them. The gro--tesque baby would grasp an evening darkness with its white, moldy palm and suck on it.

As the candle was lit, the house would become even darker, heavier. The shipwrecked house would sink toward the bottom of the night by several centimeters. As that happened, several people in the house would float up in the night. A mother doll. Now too old to be able to talk, she would rise out of the closet.

A mirror. A large mirror with its mercury peeled off. He was clinging, like a stain made by the rain, to a wall of the triangular room. A spider. A flat spider.

A staircase. A thread-like staircase you climb down to sleep. —We all, you all.

—*Emptiness*

Under the staircase I caught sight of Rabbit's ears and hands. He was engrossed in grooming his whiskers, but suddenly said, "Watch out for those people." Both Distraction and Ravage. The baby born between them is even worse.

"He grows very fast. Especially at a time like this."

He told me the baby's name was *Emptiness*. This novel name, despite Rabbit's disgust, sounded familiar to me, though I don't know why.

"You better kick him out while he's small," Rabbit said.

—He has an ugly face. You shouldn't allow him to grow all over the place.

Near daybreak, the moon happened by the window of the triangular room. The moon, already faded, reeled as she walked, but even her feeble light prevented my sleep.

The still infant *Emptiness*—that hybrid baby was crawling out of the wall. The moon's skinny fingers were pointing at his face. He indeed had an ugly, sallow face.

"Don't come near me!" Despite myself I raised my hands and tried to block the baby.

Emptiness uttered a hoarse voice and swung his skinny arms up toward me. The moon, now almost shapeless, passed inside the peeled mirror. The slightly soiled daybreak, not really worth the name of daybreak, began to color portions of the mirror.

—*Smiling Buns*

The house that had escaped the fire stiffened with its expression of amazement; before long, though, it became in its own way a familiar part of the landscape.

A shop sign that had flown over from some place in a bomb blast and cut into a utility pole remained unremoved for a long time. On a day when a strong wind blew, the tin sign made a racket, banging in the air.

When we opened the window to the west, the tin sheet was struggling almost within our reach.

Its paint had peeled off, but we still could read the letters, "Smiling Buns."

"A bun-maker's sign," Father mumbled. We had no way of telling where the shop was.

In the morning, we cooked and ate a light stew.

At noon, we ate an even lighter stew.

At night, we cooked a truly light stew.

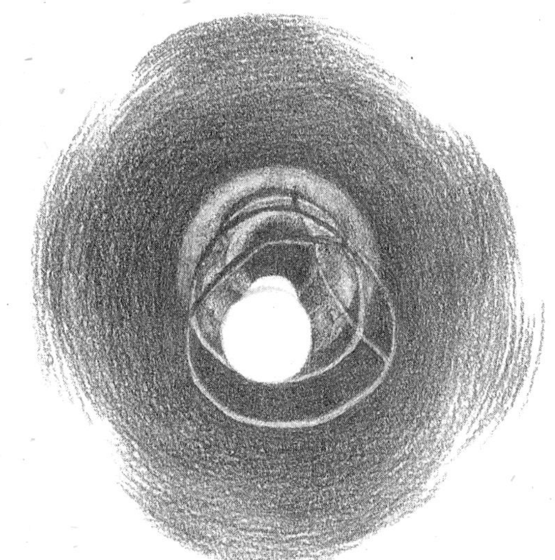

At the wildest estimate, I didn't weigh more than twenty-two pounds. Even so, we managed to ration out the rice in the pillow to ourselves until the last day of the year the war ended.

That year autumn passed by in awfully quick steps.

It was a huge, dark-brown man.

His strange arms appeared one morning in the window to the west; the next day his thick chest already blocked its sooty windowpanes.

He stared at the "Smiling Buns" sign in puzzlement and from time to time raised a hooting voice like an engine whistle.

Father would go out in the garden and pick the leaves of sweet potatoes and chamomiles, as well as wildflowers of autumn whose names he wasn't certain of. He would wash them and put them in a pot. As he sauntered in the garden, he grew skinny and brown, and looked like giant Autumn's remote relative or his illegitimate son.

On misty nights—in my memory there were many misty nights that year—as Father and I sat around the pot, I would hear the dark-brown man laugh staggeringly loud peels of laughter. Because of the voice that was so loud as to sound empty, the night felt all the more quiet, holding its breath.

Autumn grasses are tough, I thought. Autumn grasses are bitter, I thought.

Autumn passed by the window to the west, in no time showing his back. Dark-brown spots began to grow on the Smiling Buns and spread over the tin sheet day by day.

A demobilized soldier we didn't know came to visit. He came to tell us of an uncle's death. Killed in battle. In Manchuria. Twenty-four years old. Immediately after that a telegram reached us.

Another uncle's death. Died of illness. In Valley of Winds. I had thought he was old, but he was fifty-four.

Deaths came one after another. In the midst of all those deaths that I could hardly memorize, I was gazing at the Smiling Buns. The letters had become hardly legible by the time of searing winds; one night, though, the tin sheet, bathed in the moonlight and gleaming a little, reminded me of some kind of corpse. He was beautiful in his own way. Late at night, I called his name with all my heart. He has no home to return to, I thought, as I understood the unexpected end of his life.

There's a yard. A big, wide yard of a farmhouse. A well-sweep. The crepe myrtle was nearing the end of its flowering season. The sun at the end of August was deploying its bluish light in the yard and around the well. The yard still exists for certain, but can no longer be reached—by me.

Uncles died. During the war. Three of them together. Very simply.

Aunt died. All by herself. Then Grandmother. The next year, someone, who was it, died. I no longer remember their names or lineal relations. At the news of someone's death, whose turn was it, I laughed, despite myself. Why I laughed, I no longer remember that, either.

In the autumn my last uncle died, Father and I went to Valley of Winds. To arrange a release of property.

At the village limit Valley of Winds I parted with Father to be alone.

I walked through rice fields.

Each time I saw a crepe myrtle I stopped.

I crossed the river and went through an oak wood.

In the yard of a farmhouse, I inquired about "the house of the Ōshima family?"

A young wife looked at me suspiciously and asked back, "The Ōshima family?"

Once, I was given rice in that family's yard—I briefly explained, but barely conveyed to her what I really had in mind.

"Around here, everyone's called Ōshima."

She said in a voice mixing confusion and pity for me.

"You mean every family?"

"Yeah, yes. Everyone in the village is called Ōshima."

I couldn't move for a while. Finally I mustered enough courage and said.

"Well. . .it's the Ōshima family that has a crepe myrtle in their yard."

Crepe myrtle, crepe myrtle. The voice was transmitted from one mouth to another deep into the house. All the family members came out to look at me, a spectacle, each saying, "Crepe myrtle."

"She's got to mean 'laughing flowers,'" an elder said.

Laughing flowers, laughing flowers! One member after another of the family pointed at the crepe myrtle at the edge of the yard. The crepe myrtle, which had now shed all its flowers, was a figure of derision, as it stretched its arms toward the western sky.

"Around here—you see," another person said—you'd scarcely find a house without laughing flowers.

There's a yard. The crepe myrtle was about to end its flowering time. That day, I was in fourth grade, I was determined to love—love by betting the rest of my life on it. I didn't know anything about a strange word like love, yet I persisted in the resolve that I had to love.

After that I loved nothing—nothing at all.

There's a yard. There's no yard. The place is far. I no longer can see it. Even if I walked all my life, I'd never reach it.

The crepe myrtle was about to end its flowering time.
Emaciated flowers, laughing dryly, desultorily,
are scattering to the ground—no yard.

—The Eve of Ascension Day

The small town was buzzing with the Ascension Festival.

Of course it has nothing to do with the ascension of the Virgin Mary or John the Baptist. It is that of Rabbit.

Look, every vending stall has rabbit masks.

They are made with mud during the summer, all over town.

Rabbit scarves, rabbit *pochettes*—these are ordinary stuff. Shoe horns shaped like a rabbit's ears sold well one year. They're out of style now. Rabbit crackers are no good, either.

This year rabbit dishes are the main thing. They say the vendor of skewered baby rabbits, broiled, their heads attached, has had lines.

The show house for *Three-legged, Black-eyed Rabbits* is doing pretty good, too.

Don't miss the shrine hall.

All the children are wearing rabbit masks.

They play the tune of "The Hopping Rabbit" or "The Earless Rabbit." These tunes make me nostalgic.

That's all the music they have, any time.

Form a circle. Beating time with hands. Dance round and round.

An occasional somersault. —Few children can do it.

One child, who appeared to be my companion, was exceptionally good at it. As the acetylene lamp darkened, he was hopping back and forth off stage.

Am I a child? No, I must be an adult by now, I wondered, putting the design of my yukata against the lamp or doing other silly things.

"You're good at somersaulting."

When we came out of the dancing ring, I said to the child, though I hadn't meant to.

"Well . . . yes."

"Where did you learn it?"

"I didn't . . . I seem to be born this way."

The moon had started to rise. In its light he turned to look at me.

What a let-down, he was a real rabbit.

"Times are bad," he said. "Unless you *pretend* to be wearing a mask, you end up being made into rabbit stew."

We sang the song of "The Earless Rabbit" as we walked the road beneath the embankment. From time to time he touched his ears worriedly.

The autumn and the moon had dyed him bronze.

At a small pub outside the town we ordered vegetable plates.

For it was the only place where there were no rabbit dishes on the menu.

"Once," said Rabbit.

"It was long ago, there was a war. This town also had an air raid and was surrounded by fires. I tell you, it was terrible. Burning a small rural town like this, well, I bet the other side had an awful lot of excess bombs."

"Were you born by then?"

"Sort of, yes." He hastily smoothed his whiskers. Then, remembering that he was *pretending* to be wearing a mask, he even more hastily put a napkin around his neck.

"Incendiary bombs were scattered to the east, to the west, to the south, to the north. Forming a circle, you see. Then the fires would slowly gather toward the center. It's called a 'frying pan' tactic. You had no place to escape to. At that moment, out of nowhere a rabbit showed up. All the people followed him. You see, there was no other choice. So, they walked through the abandoned underground water main and came out on the riverbed. The result was, lots of people were saved."

"You mean, this festival is in gratitude for that?"

"Yep, right. They built a statue for me, too. There are rabbit cakes, rabbit sweets."

"But aren't you troubled by rabbit dishes?"

"It's the age, you see. Not gratitude, but the auspicious sense has remained. Someone has come up with the idea of rabbit pies, I hear. He's now applying for a patent on it, they say."

In every crossroads, the small town was full of high-pitched, lovely voices of children.

Ascension, Ascension, they called to one another.

Rabbit, Rabbit, ascend to Heaven!

As we reached Town Hall, my companion visibly shrank. On the Monument for War Victims he turned pale and stiffened.

In Town Hall, a lecture with the lengthy title of "Rabbit: The One Who Came for the Sake of Peace," was about to start. There was clapping of hands, deepening the autumn and the night.

author, translator, artist

Reiko Koyanagi, who was born in Tokyo, in 1935,
established Tokiwa Gallery in 1964
and started publication of the Mujinkan
(Dreamer's Pavilion) series of art books in 1988.
Among the artists she has published
in that series so far are Frida Kahlo, Richard Dadd,
Mendelssohn, Jean Delville, and Richard Oelze.
She started publishing books of poems in 1966.
Her fifth book, here translated
Rabbit of the Nether World,
won the Poets' Club prize in 1990.

Hiroaki Sato, born in Taiwan, in 1945,
and a resident of New York since 1968,
has published two dozen books of Japanese poetry
in English translation. A book of his own poems,
Six Renga on Love & Other Poems,
was published by St. Andrews Press, in 1988.
He is now at work on an anthology
of Japanese women poets from ancient to modern times.

Monica Tamano, born in Tokyo, in 1966,
and baptized in 1991 (hence her name Monica),
has exhibited her work in a variety of shows since 1994.
At present she works at Koyanagi's gallery Mujinkan.

colophon

Set in 12/14 Palatino,
with Zapf Chancery titles and headers.

Cover is Fox River Filare #80 Pompeii Ash;
endsheet is Curtis Crown Vantage #60 Natural Crepe;
textsheet is Fox River EverGreen #70 Aspen Cord.

Design by Jim Kacian for Red Moon Press,
Winchester VA.

Printed and bound by Bookmasters, Inc.,
Mansfield OH.